Penguin Readers

WONDER

R.J. PALACIO

LEVEL

3

RETOLD BY NICK BULLARD
ILLUSTRATED BY GUY HARVEY
SERIES EDITOR: SORREL PITTS

PENGUIN BOOKS

UK | USA | Canada | Ireland | Australia
India | New Zealand | South Africa

Penguin Books is part of the Penguin Random House group of companies
whose addresses can be found at global.penguinrandomhouse.com.
www.penguin.co.uk www.puffin.co.uk www.ladybird.co.uk

Penguin
Random House
UK

Wonder first published in Great Britain by The Bodley Head, 2012
Penguin Readers edition of *Wonder* published by Penguin Books Ltd, 2019
001

Original text written by R. J. Palacio
Text for Penguin Readers edition adapted by Nick Bullard
Text copyright © R. J. Palacio, 2012
Illustrated by Guy Harvey
Illustrations copyright © Penguin Books Ltd, 2019
Cover illustration copyright © Tad Carpenter, 2012

The moral right of the original author and the original illustrator has been asserted

Printed and bound in Great Britain by Clays Ltd, Elcograf S.p.A.

A CIP catalogue record for this book is available from the British Library

ISBN: 978-0-241-39789-3

All correspondence to:
Penguin Books
Penguin Random House Children's
80 Strand, London WC2R 0RL

Contents

People in the story

August

Via

Mom

Dad

Jack

Summer

Miranda

Justin

New words

flashlight

hearing aid

high-five

hug

mask

medal

puppy

violin

Note about the story

R.J. Palacio's parents came from Colombia, but she was born in New York, in 1963. She worked as an artist for many years, drawing pictures for books and book covers. The idea for *Wonder* came to her one day when she was in an ice cream store in New York with her two sons, and they were standing next to a boy with a very different face. Her younger son looked at the boy and started to cry because he was frightened. Palacio was worried, and she and her sons left the store quickly. When they got home, she was angry with herself because she did not talk to the boy. She did not show her sons that there was nothing to be afraid of.

She started to think about the boy, and asked herself questions about his life every day. She wrote *Wonder* to try to answer those questions. *Wonder* was made into a movie in 2017.

Before-reading question

1 Look at the cover of the book, then look quickly at the pictures in the book. Which sentences are true, do you think?
   a August lives on a farm.
   b August lives with his grandparents.
   c August has an easy life at school.

*Definitions of words in **bold** can be found in the glossary on pages 77–80.

CHAPTER ONE

Why I didn't go to school

August

I know I'm not an **ordinary*** ten-year-old **kid**. I do ordinary things. I eat ice cream. I ride my bike. I have an Xbox. And I feel ordinary inside. But ordinary children run away from me in the playground. And ordinary people **stare** at me in the street or at the supermarket.

I walk down the street and people look at me, and then they look away.

My older sister, Via, doesn't think I'm ordinary. She gets angry if people talk about me or if they stare at me. She shouts at them. She loves me, but she doesn't think I'm ordinary.

Mom and Dad don't think I'm ordinary, either. They think that I'm **extraordinary**.

I think I *am* ordinary, but nobody sees it.

Mom is beautiful, and so is Via. And Dad is handsome. My name is August. What do I look like? I'm not going to tell you. But it's worse than you think. Here's something not ordinary about me: I have never been to school. People think

I haven't been to school because of the way that I look. But it isn't that. It's because I've been in hospital a lot—twenty-seven times in ten years. I've had a lot of **plastic surgery** and other things. So, my parents didn't send me to school. Mom taught me at home.

My last visit to hospital was eight months ago, and I don't have to go back for two years.

One day this summer, I heard my parents talking about schools.

"What are you talking about?" I asked.

"Do you think you're ready for school?" asked Mom.

"No," I said.

"I can't teach you much more," she said. "You know I am bad at **math**."

"What school?" I asked.

"Beecher Prep. Near our house."

"I really don't want to," I said.

"OK," said Mom. "We'll talk about it later."

I didn't want to go. But I knew Mom was right. And she is really bad at math.

———

In the summer vacation, we went to the school to see the school **principal**, Mr. Tushman.

"Hi, Mr. Tushman, nice to see you again," said Mom. "This is my son, August."

Mr. Tushman **shook** Mom's hand, and then mine.

"Hi, August," said Mr. Tushman. He looked at me. Not many people do that. "I'm very happy to meet you. Your mom and dad have told me a lot about you."

"What have they told you?"

"That you like to read. That you're a great artist. And that you really like **science**. Is that right?"

"Yes," I said. "I do."

"We have some great science teachers here," said Mr. Tushman. "Now, you need to visit the school."

I liked Mr. Tushman.

Outside the door of Mr. Tushman's office I could hear children's voices. Suddenly, I was frightened again. I'm OK with little children. Sometimes they say **cruel** things, but they don't want to hurt you. But older children are more difficult. So, I have long hair because then I can't see things if I don't want to.

"August," said Mr. Tushman, "I want you to meet some other fifth-**grade** students."

"I don't want to meet any kids," I said to Mom.

Mr. Tushman looked into my eyes. "This is going to be OK, August," he said. "These are nice people." And he opened the door.

"Come in, children," he said, and two boys and a girl walked in. They didn't look at me or Mom. They stood near the door and looked at Mr. Tushman. They were frightened, too.

"Thank you for coming," said Mr. Tushman.

"I want you to meet August, a new student. He'll be in your **homeroom**. So, this is August. August, this is Jack."

Jack looked at me and put out his hand. I shook it. He smiled, said "Hey," and looked down quickly.

"This is Julian," said Mr. Tushman.

Julian did the same as Jack. He shook my hand, smiled and looked down.

"And Charlotte."

Charlotte had really blonde hair. She didn't shake my hand, but she waved and smiled. "Hi, August. Nice to meet you," she said.

"Hi," I said, looking down. She had green shoes.

"OK," said Mr. Tushman. "Maybe you can show the school to August. Take him to your homeroom, and then show him the science room and the computer room. Don't forget the **cafeteria**."

The three children went out the room. I had to follow them.

Jack, Julian, Charlotte, and I walked across a hall and up some stairs. Nobody said a word. We stopped at a door with the number 301 on it.

"This is our homeroom," said Julian. "We have Ms. Petosa. She's OK."

Julian walked down the hall. He stopped at another door and opened it a little. "This is the science room." He stood in front of the door, and he didn't look at me. "The best science teacher is Mr. Haller."

"Open the door more so August can see inside," said Jack, and he pushed the door some more. Julian moved out the way quickly because he didn't want to touch me. But he pointed to some of the things in the room. "That big thing is the **board**. Those are desks, and those are chairs."

"I'm sure he knows that," said Charlotte.

"I have a question," I said. "What is homeroom?"

"It's your group. You go there in the morning," said Charlotte. "Your homeroom teacher checks that everybody is in school. You see her every day. Do you understand?"

"Yes, thanks," I said.

Next, they showed me the theater—Charlotte's favorite place—and the library.

Then, Julian said, "Can I ask a question?"

"OK," I said.

"Why is your face like that? Were you in a fire?"

"Julian!" said Charlotte. "You can't ask that. He was born like that. Mr. Tushman told us. You weren't listening!"

"Come on, August," said Jack. He opened the library door and looked me in the face. I looked back at him and smiled. He smiled, too. "Julian's a **jerk**," he said, quietly.

———

"Were they nice to you?" asked Mom, at home.

"Jack was OK," I said, "but not Julian."

"You don't have to go to school if you don't want to," Mom said.

"It's OK, Mom. I want to." It was true.

CHAPTER TWO
School

August

I was **nervous** on my first day of school. Mom and Dad were nervous, too. They took a lot of pictures of me and Via. Via is fourteen, and it was her first day, too, at her new high school.

Beecher Prep isn't a long way from our house, but I didn't often go near it. I like to stay nearer home because the people in our street know me.

We all walked down Amesfort Avenue. Via walked next to me, and Mom and Dad walked behind us. Then, we turned a corner, and we saw children in front of the school—hundreds of them, talking, or standing with their parents. I kept my head down.

"Remember, it's the first day," said Via in my ear. "Everyone's nervous."

Mr. Tushman was in front of the school, talking to parents and students. One or two girls looked at me and then looked away, but that was all right.

"OK, big boy," said Dad.

"Have a great first day," said Via. She kissed and **hugged** me.

Mom and Dad hugged me, too. Mom was going to cry, so I turned and ran into the school.

I went up to room 301. There were some children in homeroom already, and Ms. Petosa was writing on the board. I found a desk near the middle at the back and sat down. More children came in and sat down, but nobody sat next to me.

"Hi, August." It was Charlotte. She waved. I saw Julian, too, and he saw me. But he didn't speak to me.

Someone sat next to me. It was Jack.

"Hi, August."

"Hi, Jack." I waved, and then I felt stupid. Waving isn't **cool**.

After homeroom, the first class was English, in room 321. I walked there quickly and sat at the back. The teacher was writing on the board. Again, nobody sat next to me — but then Jack did. He was talking and laughing with some other children. He had a lot of friends. I looked around the room. Charlotte and Julian were in this class, too.

Everyone went quiet, and the teacher, Mr. Browne, started to talk. Then, he wrote a word on the board: *PRECEPT*.

"What does 'precept' mean? Who knows?" he asked.

Nobody put up a hand.

He wrote again: *PRECEPTS — IMPORTANT THINGS TO REMEMBER*.

"Well," he asked. "What are the important things?"

Some hands went up, and Mr. Browne wrote some students' ideas on the board:

HOMEWORK. FAMILY. PARENTS.

Soon, there were a lot of words on the board. Then, he wrote this:

MR. BROWNE'S SEPTEMBER PRECEPT:
IT IS BETTER TO BE KIND THAN RIGHT.

"In your books, write the date, and then write this precept by Dr. Wayne W. Dyer," Mr. Browne told us. "I'll give you a new precept every month, and we'll talk about it. And, at the end of the year, in the summer vacation, you can write your own precepts and send them to me."

I wrote down the September precept. "I think that I'm going to like school," I thought.

Lunch was *really* hard. Everybody ran into the cafeteria at the same time, talking loudly and choosing seats. I sat at an empty table and waited. I had a sandwich and a drink in my bag, so I didn't need to stand in line for school food.

Eating isn't easy for me. I've had a lot of plastic surgery on my mouth, but it's still not right, and it looks strange. Some of the children in the cafeteria were staring at me. I didn't look at them, but I knew.

"Is this seat free?"

A girl was standing by my table, holding her lunch.

"Yes," I said.

She put her lunch on the table and sat down across from me. She had a school burger and cheese, and she started to eat.

"Yuck," she said. "You were right to bring a sandwich."

"Yes."

"My name's Summer," she said. "What's yours?"

"August."

"Cool."

"Summer!" Another girl came over. "Why are you sitting here? Come to our table."

"There are too many people there. Come and sit here," Summer said.

"They're all waiting for me," said the girl, and she walked away.

Summer looked at me, smiled, and ate some more burger.

"Our names go together," she said. "Summer. August."

"Oh, yes," I said.

"We can make this the summer table. Only people with summer names can sit here. Is there anyone in fifth grade called June or July?" she asked.

"There's a Maya in my homeroom," I said.

"May is really in spring. But I guess it's OK if she wants to sit here. There's Julian: that's like July."

I didn't say anything.

"Mr. Browne teaches our English class," I said.

"Why is that like summer?"

"When you go in the sun, you get brown," I replied.

"OK," she said. "And what about Ms. Petosa? I think petosa is a flower, so it's a summer thing."

"I have Ms. Petosa for homeroom," I said.

"I have her for math," said Summer. "I don't like her much."

By the end of lunch, we had the names of ten children and teachers for the summer table.

"Is Jack a summer name?" I asked.

Summer thought for a second. "No," she said. "But if someone has a winter name and wants to be on the summer table, that's OK."

"Cool," I said.

Summer looked like her name. Her face was brown, and she had green summer eyes.

CHAPTER THREE
Halloween

August

Mom always asks me how something feels: between one and ten. It started in hospital two years ago, after some surgery on my mouth. They took some **bone** from my leg to put in my face —to make me look more ordinary. So, my face hurt, and my leg hurt, and I couldn't open my mouth to talk. *One* meant it hurt just a little, and *ten* meant it hurt a lot.

After school, Mom was waiting for me outside. She hugged me and said, "How was it? One to ten?"

"Five," I said.

She was surprised. "That's good!"

We started to walk home.

"See you tomorrow, August!" It was Summer. She was crossing the street.

"Bye, Summer," I said, waving to her.

"Who was that?" asked Mom, after a minute.

"Summer."

"Is she in your homeroom?"

"No," I replied.

"Did you like your teachers?"

"Yes."

"What about Julian, Jack, and Charlotte?" she asked.

"I sat next to Jack a lot."

"How did you meet Summer?" asked Mom.

"We sat together at lunch," I said.

"She looks nice."

"She is."

"And she's pretty."

"Yes," I said. "We're like ***Beauty and the Beast***."

September was hard. It wasn't easy to get up early in the morning. And homework was a new idea for me. I didn't have any free time. Before, I could play a lot, but I couldn't do that now.

And school was really difficult. In every new class I met new children, and they stared at me. They tried not to stare, but I knew. And in the classroom and the halls they walked around me.

They weren't cruel. They didn't say horrible things. They just wanted to look. And sometimes I wanted to say, "It's OK, you can look."

After about one week, the children in my classes

knew about me, and after two weeks, everyone in fifth grade did. After a month, the children in the other grades did, too. These were big children of twelve or thirteen. Some of them had strange hair, or rings in their noses. But none of them looked like me.

I sat next to Jack in a lot of classes, and we had a great time. Jack was always laughing. One day, in class, Jack smiled and asked me, quietly, "August, are you always going to look like this? Can't you get plastic surgery or something?"

I smiled. "This is after plastic surgery!"

"You really need to find a new doctor!" said Jack, and we both laughed a lot. The teacher came over,

told us to be quiet, and moved us to different desks.

Mr. Browne's precept for October was:

PEOPLE REMEMBER YOU BECAUSE OF WHAT YOU DO.

Someone wrote this thousands of years ago, in Egypt, Mr. Browne told us.

Most of the children at school were nice to me, but they didn't want to go too near me. In class, they talked to me, but they didn't sit next to me. And they walked around me because they didn't want to touch me.

My birthday is October 10th. I like that: 10/10.

I usually have a little party at home, but this year I wanted a bigger party. I wanted to go **bowling** with some friends.

"Who do you want to ask?" asked Mom.

"Everyone in my homeroom, and Summer," I replied.

"That's a lot of people."

"I know," I said. "But I can't **invite** some people from my homeroom and not others."

"OK," said Mom. "I'll email all the parents."

A week later, I was at home in the living room. I was playing with our dog, Daisy. She's old, now, but we all love her. She likes to sleep on my bed, and I like to hug her and have her near me. I talked to Mom about my birthday.

"Who is coming to the party?" I asked her.

"Jack, Summer, Reid, the two Maxes. Charlotte has a dance class, but she will come if there's time. And Tristan has a soccer game; he'll try to come after that."

"Is that all?" I said. "That's only five people!"

"We asked late," she explained. "And a lot of children had other things to do."

"Why isn't Julian coming?"

"Julian's mom didn't answer. So, I don't know."

My birthday party was small, but a lot of my uncles and aunts came. The adults were bowling next to the children, and we all had a great time.

————

I didn't see Summer much in class, but we always sat at our summer table for lunch. At lunch the day after my birthday, Summer asked me about **Halloween**.

"You can wear a **costume** to school, you know," she told me.

"That's cool," I replied. "Maybe I'll go as Boba Fett from *Star Wars*. What about you?"

"I guess I'll go in black—as a **witch**."

Halloween is the best holiday for me. It's better than Christmas because I can wear a costume and a **mask**. Nobody looks at me. I'd like to have Halloween every day.

On the morning of Halloween, I put on my Boba Fett costume. On the way into school, I passed someone with the same costume. We looked at one another, and he **high-fived** me. He didn't know it was me, of course.

In homeroom, everybody was in costume, with masks. I heard Julian's voice; he was talking to three other boys. "He doesn't need a mask,"

he said to them. "He looks horrible without one."

The other boys laughed. I knew that Julian was talking about me.

"Why do you sit next to him all the time?" Julian asked one of the boys.

"I don't know." It was Jack's voice. "Mr. Tushman asked me to be nice to him. And now he always wants to be with me."

I ran to the bathroom. I stayed there for a few minutes, and then went to see the school nurse. "My stomach hurts," I told her, and she **called** Mom. Mom came into school and took me home.

The next day was Friday, and I didn't go to school. I had the weekend to think about things, but I was sure of one thing: I wasn't going back to school.

CHAPTER FOUR

My brother, August

Via

August is at the center of the family, and we all understand that.

I'm OK with it. I know that August is special. I know that his face hurt after plastic surgery, and he needed to sleep. So, I always played quietly. I wanted Mom and Dad to watch me play soccer. But usually it wasn't possible, because they were taking August to the hospital or to a new doctor.

"You're the kindest girl in the world," Mom and Dad said to me. I don't know if that is true. But I don't **complain**. I've seen August in hospital after surgery, and he looks terrible. So, how could I complain because I didn't get a new toy, or Mom didn't come to the school **play**?

It's been like this all my life. But it's changing now, I think.

———

I loved middle school because it was different from home. I was Olivia there, not Via. Via is my name at home. And in middle school a lot of people didn't know about August. I'm always going to have a brother with problems, and I love August. But I want to be Olivia, not August's sister.

Now, I'm at high school, and the best thing about it is that *nobody* knows me. The only people I knew already were Miranda and Ella. I've always been friends with them. So, they've always known August, too. Miranda has been like another sister to August. She always played with him a lot, and they loved to sing together.

Miranda, Ella, and I were together all through middle school. We were so excited about going to high school together. But we're in high school now, and things are very different.

This summer, Miranda didn't call me after summer **camp**. "Maybe she stayed longer," I thought, but then I looked at Facebook. She was already home, but she didn't call or **text** me. I texted her, and she texted back, but we didn't meet.

I met Miranda and Ella on the first day of high school. Miranda looked very different. Her hair was short, and bright pink, and her clothes were different. She acted differently, too. She was friendly, but not very friendly. We all sat together at lunch, and she and Ella talked a lot. I didn't

say much. I didn't feel that I was in the group any more.

"We're driving you home today," said Miranda, at the end of school. "Your mom called. She has to be with August."

"Thanks, but I'm OK," I said. I didn't want to sit in a car with the new Miranda, so I went home on the bus.

The bus took a long time, and I got home late.

"Hi, Via," said Mom, as soon as I came in. "How was your first day?"

"OK."

"Is Miranda with you?" she asked.

"No," I said, "she can't stay. We have a lot of homework."

"Really? On your first day?" Mom said.

"Yes, really!" I shouted. "How was August's first day?"

"OK," she said, slowly.

"What does that mean? Good or bad?" I asked. I was getting angrier.

"Good, I think. Via, what's wrong?"

"Nothing!" I ran to my room and closed the door.

Mom came into my room after dinner. She looked tired.

"What's the matter, Via?" she asked.

"Not now, OK?" I said.

"I'll come back at bedtime," Mom said.

She didn't come back, but Dad did.

"Mom's with August," he said. "Goodnight." And he kissed me.

_____

August usually loves Halloween. But this year he came home, ran to the bathroom, and **threw up**. Then he went to bed. At 7 p.m., I went to see him. He was on the bed, looking at the wall.

"What's the matter?" I asked.

"Nothing," he said.

"Is it school?"

"Yes."

"Teachers? Homework? Friends?"

He told me about Jack and Julian. "They said cruel things about me. I thought Jack was my friend," he said.

August didn't go to school on Friday. On Sunday, I talked to him again.

"I'm not going to school tomorrow," he said. "I hate school. I'm never going back."

"August," I said, "you must go. We all have bad days sometimes. You heard Jack and Julian, but they don't know that. That's great. Don't talk to them, and they won't know why. Or act like a friend, but you know inside that you're not."

"Like you and Miranda?" he said.

"What?" I said.

"Miranda called me," he told me. "You're not friends, she says, but she's still my big sister."

I couldn't speak for a minute. Then, I asked, "Did Miranda say anything about me?"

"Yes," he replied. "She **misses** you."

August did go to school on Monday.

CHAPTER FIVE
"He's a nice kid"

Summer

Some kids are so strange.

"Why are you friends with 'the **freak**?'" they ask me.

"He's a nice kid," I say. "And he's not a freak."

"You're a good person," said Ximena. "I couldn't do that."

"Did Mr. Tushman ask you to be his friend?" asked Charlotte.

"No. I want to be friends with him," I said.

I sat with August the first day because I was sorry for him. No one was talking to him. He looks very strange, but he's just a kid.

It's true; it isn't easy to look at August's face. We always have lunch together, and he doesn't eat very well. But he's nice. I don't feel sorry for him now. I sit with him because he's interesting.

This year, the other kids only want to sit and talk after lunch. They don't want to play any more. And they talk about who likes who, and who is **cute**. August isn't interested in that.

He likes to play **four square**. I love four square, too.

One day, I was talking to Maya. "Don't touch August," she said.

"Why?" I asked.

"You'll get 'the **plague**.' If you touch August, you must wash your hands in thirty seconds. Or you'll get the plague. Everyone says so."

"That's stupid," I said.

"I know," said Maya. "But I don't want to touch a ball after August has touched it."

Another day, I was talking to Savanna.

"How's your **boyfriend**?" she asked.

"Who?" I said.

"August."

"He's not my boyfriend."

"I know," she said. "But why are you with a freak all the time?"

"He's not a freak," I replied.

"Julian really likes you. He wants to ask you out."

"Does he?"

"Yes," she said. "He's really cute. But you have to choose. It's Julian or the freak."

————————

August wasn't at school the day after Halloween, but we had lunch together the next Monday. He was very quiet, and he didn't look at me.

"What's the matter, August?" I asked.

"You know, Summer," he said, "you don't need to be with me."

"What?"

"You're nice to me because Mr. Tushman asked you to be," he said.

"No!" I shouted.

"He did."

"He did not! August, I **promise**."

"Really?"

"Really!" I was angry now.

"OK. I'm sorry, Summer."

He told me about Julian and Jack at Halloween. "But don't tell anyone," he said.

"I promise," I replied.

———————

Before August came to my house for the first time, I told Mom about his face. But, when she came home from work and saw him, she *was* surprised.

"Hi, Mom. This is August. Can he stay for dinner?" I said.

"Hi, August," she said. "Of course."

"Don't stare at him!" I **whispered** to her.

After that, she was really nice to August.

We went to my room to do some homework. Then, we went into the living room. August was looking at some family pictures on the wall, and one of them was of me and my dad.

"Is that your dad?" he asked.

"Yes," I said.

"I didn't know he was black. I never see him outside school."

"He died five years ago. He was a soldier," I said.

"I'm sorry, Summer," August said. "I didn't know."

"It's not easy. I miss him a lot."

After that, August and I were together a lot after school. Mom and I had dinner at August's house twice. His parents are cool, and Mom liked them, too.

One day at school, Jack asked me a question.

"Summer," he asked, "is August angry with me? He never talks to me."

"Yes," I said. "But I can't say why. I promised."

"Can you help me? Give me a little idea?" he said.

I looked at him. I promised August, but I was sorry for Jack. He's a nice kid.

"Halloween mask," I whispered in his ear.

CHAPTER SIX
Friends and enemies

Jack

In the middle of last summer, Mr. Tushman called my parents. I heard Mom talking to him.

"What was that about?" I asked.

"They have a new kid at school," Mom said. "He doesn't know the school, and they want someone to help him."

"Why me?" I asked.

"Because you're a nice kid," said Mom. "And this boy has something wrong with his face."

"No, I can't do it, Mom!" I said.

I knew it was a kid called August. I saw him sometimes in the street. He looked terrible. One day, I was with my seven-year-old brother Jamie. We saw August, and Jamie was very frightened.

"Did Mr. Tushman ask any other kids?" I asked.

"Yes. Julian and Charlotte. They said yes."

"Julian!" I shouted. "He's a jerk. He'll be horrible to a kid like that. Mom, I know this kid. He's called August, and he looks terrible."

Jamie came into the kitchen to get a drink.

"Jamie," I said. "Do you remember that kid we saw? His face frightened you."

"Yes," said Jamie. "I shouted and ran away. He was so ugly." Jamie started to run about, holding his head and shouting.

Mom didn't say anything. She just looked at me.

"OK," I said. "Call Mr. Tushman. I'll do it."

Why did I agree? It wasn't because of Julian. There are always jerks. It was because of Jamie running about and shouting. Jamie's a nice kid. So, if nice kids are cruel like that, August needs help.

After the surprise the first few times you see it, August's face is OK. And he's a really nice kid; he's very funny and easy to talk to. He's smart, like Charlotte and Ximena, and he helps me with homework. (They don't!) At first, I was his friend because Mr. Tushman asked me. But, now, I want us to be friends. But it was strange. One day August and I were friends, and the next day he wasn't talking to me.

"August, are you angry with me?" I asked. He walked away.

And it was hard because we sat together in most classes. Science was really difficult now, and he didn't help me any more.

One day, I asked Summer, "Is August angry with me?" She stared at me for a moment before she answered.

"Halloween mask," she said.

I didn't understand. Then, I remembered: the

Halloween costumes in homeroom. I was talking to Julian. August was there, and I didn't know it because of his mask. I suddenly felt very sick.

Later that day, in science, I sat next to August, and we didn't speak. I wanted to, but what could I say?

At the end of the class, Ms. Rubin gave us our homework.

"You do this in groups of two," she said. "Charlotte and Ximena; August and Jack . . ."

After class, Julian came to talk to me.

"Jack, do you want to work with me?" he asked. "You don't want to work with that freak."

I hit him hard, in the mouth.

———————

The next day, Mom and I were in Mr. Tushman's office.

"Jack, this is very bad," he said. "We may ask you to leave the school. Why did you hit Julian?"

"I can't say," I replied.

"Jack, you must. I need to understand."

I didn't speak.

"OK," said Mr. Tushman. Was he smiling? "It's Christmas vacation next week. You go home, and write me a letter to explain. And write Julian a letter to say sorry. And I'll see you in the New Year."

December 18th

Dear Mr. Tushman,
    I am very, very sorry for hitting Julian. I can't tell you why I hit him, but it was very wrong. I know that. I am writing a letter to Julian, too.
                Yours,
                Jack Will

December 18th

Dear Julian,
    I am very sorry for hitting you. It was wrong of me. I hope your mouth is better soon.
                Yours,
                Jack Will

December 26th

Dear Jack,
    Thank you for your letter. It was wrong to hit Julian. But I think that I understand a little.
                Laurence Tushman

Hi August, it's Jack. I want to say sorry. You're angry with me, and I know why. I said something stupid.

But it's not true—I don't think that. I'm sorry.

I got your message. Did Summer tell you?

She said, "Halloween mask," and I guessed.

Did you really hit Julian?

Yes. In the mouth.

Why?

I don't know.

Did he say something about me?

Julian's a jerk. I'm really sorry. Please can we be friends again?

OK.

Great!

I went back to school in January, and things were very strange. The first kid I met was Amos. Amos is not one of my friends, but he's always been friendly to me. I said "Hi," and he looked at me and walked away.

Then, I saw Henry and said "Hi," but he walked away. It was the same with Tristan.

"Have I got the plague now?" I thought.

The girls talked to me, so the problem was with the boys. Only the two Maxes and August talked to me.

Then, at lunch, nobody sat with me. I went to the library and read a book.

I found a **note** in my bag at the end of the day:
Meet me in room 301 after school. Charlotte.

Charlotte was waiting for me.

"Jack, I feel bad," she said. "You need to know something. But don't tell anyone."

"Promise."

"Julian's parents had a huge party at Christmas. They invited 200 people: parents and kids. Julian talked to everyone and complained about you. You hit him because you have problems in the head, he thinks. And that's because you're friends with August. It makes things very difficult for you."

"What?" I said.

"And Julian's mom isn't happy with the school. It's not the right school for August, she says, because he has **difficulties** with learning. He must leave."

"But August is fine," I said. "He has no difficulties. You know that."

"I know," she replied. "And Julian talked to the boys. They won't talk to you."

"That's OK," I said. "They're not my friends."

Charlotte opened the door to room 301 and looked out. There was nobody outside, and she left quickly.

The next day at lunch, I sat down at a table with Tristan and Pablo. They stood up and walked away.

"Hi, Jack!" It was Summer. She and August were sitting at their table.

"Sit with us, Jack," she said.

I told them about Julian's holiday party. "He has turned the whole class against me. People don't talk to me. It's like I'm not there."

"Welcome to my world!" said August.

One evening, I was at August's house. We were playing video games. His sister, Via, came up to his bedroom. "August, I have a friend. I want you to meet him," she said.

The friend was a cool boy with glasses and long hair. He shook our hands.

"This is Justin," said Via.

"Cool room," said Justin.

He was carrying a long **case**.

"Is that a machine gun?" I asked.

"Justin plays **violin** in a zydeco band," said Via. "That's music from Louisiana."

"You should tell people that's a machine gun," said August. "Are you Via's boyfriend?"

Via smiled and pushed August's hat over his eyes. Via and Justin left the room. I looked at August, and we laughed.

CHAPTER SEVEN
The violin

Justin

I started **going out with** Olivia two months ago, and I really like her. She told me about August before I went to her house. But the first time I saw him was still a big surprise. He was with a friend, Jack. I shook their hands and tried not to look at August's face.

"Is that a machine gun?" Jack asked me. He was looking at my violin case.

"Are you Via's boyfriend?" asked August. Olivia pushed his hat over his eyes. We left the room, and I heard them laughing.

"What do you think?" Olivia asked.

"About August?"

"Yes."

"Nothing," I said. "Cool kid, I think."

"A lot of my friends don't want to come to my house," she said. "Because of August."

"It's no problem for me," I said. "I'm not frightened."

Olivia's parents invited me to dinner at a Mexican restaurant in Amesfort Avenue. I was nervous. I got to the restaurant and saw them all inside. Her dad got up and shook my hand. Her mom hugged me, and so did Olivia. And August high-fived me.

I really liked her parents. We talked a lot, and they asked about my music. They wanted to come and listen to my band. My parents never talk to me like this. My parents don't live together, and they aren't interested in my life.

After dinner, we went back to Olivia's house for ice cream, and I met their dog, Daisy. Her family says "I love you" a lot. Nobody in my family says that. Olivia and I were both in the school play. I had a big part, but she only had a small part. The biggest part for a girl went to that girl with pink hair, Miranda. Olivia was OK with having a small part, and she helped me to learn my words. I had a lot of words, and I only had six weeks.

One evening in March, we worked on my words for the play. I was leaving Olivia's house at the same time as Jack.

"Justin," said Olivia's mom, "can you walk to the bus stop with Jack, and wait for the bus with him?"

"Of course!" I said.

We walked to the bus stop.

"You don't need to stay," said Jack. "I can wait by myself."

"That's OK," I said. We got to the stop, and there were eight minutes before the bus.

"Can I borrow a dollar?" he asked. "I want to buy some candy."

I gave him a dollar, and he crossed the road and went into a store. Three boys were walking past, and they saw Jack. He came out the store, and they followed him, making strange animal noises.

Jack came back to the bus stop. "What's happening?" I asked him.

"They do it all the time. Because of my best friend."

I understood. It was hard for August, but it was hard for Jack, too.

The bus came, and Jack got on. I walked down the street and turned the corner. The three boys were there, laughing and eating ice cream.

I remembered Jack and August talking about my violin case. I took off my glasses, and held the violin case like a gun. Then I walked up to them.

"Listen, you three," I said in my James Bond voice. "Stay away from Jack or you may have an accident." I looked at my case. "Understand?"

Some ice cream fell to the ground. The boys didn't speak. I walked away quickly and didn't look back.

———

One evening, we were working on the play at school, and I was talking to Miranda.

"How long have you been going out with Olivia?" she asked.

"About four months," I replied.

"Have you met August?"

"Do you know Olivia's brother?" I asked.

"Yes," she said. "Olivia and I were good friends at middle school. I know August well. The world has been cruel to him."

CHAPTER EIGHT
Hearing aids

August

At school, the "**war**" went on into February. Only one or two kids spoke to Jack and me. We got a lot of notes. There were notes to Jack:

You smell of cheese.

Nobody likes you.

And notes to me:

Freak.

Get out of our school.

It was worse for Jack than it was for me. They took his bag or stole his homework.

But, in March, things got better. Some of Julian's friends weren't helping him any more. Then, Julian told a really stupid story.

"Jack found a hit man, with a machine gun," he told people. "He came after me, and Miles, and Henry."

This was the end of the war for most people. They stopped playing the plague game, too.

One day, I was talking to Maya and Ellie. Maya had a bag with a picture of an Uglydoll on it.

"Did you know," I asked, "that they used pictures of me to make the first Uglydoll?"

For a minute, they thought it was true. Then, they looked at me and laughed. "You're so funny, August."

The next day I found a very small Uglydoll on my chair with a nice note.

To the best August doll.
Love, Maya.

People were nice about my **hearing aids**, too.

I have never heard very well, and now I needed hearing aids. But they were horrible. My ears are very small, so the hearing aids can't go inside. They go around the back of my head, so now I cannot wear my hat any more.

"I'm not wearing these, Mom," I said.

"Wait," said the doctor. "I'll turn them on."

Wow! The hearing aids were great. I could hear everything.

The day I wore the hearing aids to school for the first time, I was worried. But it was OK. Summer was happy because I could hear better.

"You look cool, like a secret policeman," Jack told me.

———

Via was in the play at her school. She told Mom and Dad only a week before it started. With my new ears, I heard everything.

"Why didn't you tell us before?" asked Mom.

"I don't say anything in the play," said Via. "You don't need to see it."

"But Justin has a big part," said Mom. "Can't we see him?"

"No. I don't want you there," she replied.

Then, they started talking quietly, and I couldn't hear them.

Later, at dinner, I asked, "Are we going to see Justin in a play?"

"Dad's going," said Mom. "It's not a play for children, so you and I are going to stay home."

"I don't believe you," I said. "We're not going because Via doesn't want me there. She doesn't want her friends to see a freak."

I ran to my room and shut the door.

After an hour, the door opened, and Via came in. "August," she said. "Come quickly. Mom needs to talk to you."

"I'm not going to say sorry," I said.

"It's not about you!" said Via. "It's about Daisy. She's very sick." Via was crying.

In the kitchen, Daisy was on the floor. Mom was next to Daisy, and she was crying, too.

"I'm taking Daisy to the animal hospital," Mom told me. "And I don't think she's coming back. She's old, and she's very sick. You need to say goodbye, August."

The taxi was in the street, and Mom carried Daisy out.

"Goodbye, Daisy," said Via, kissing her.

"Goodbye, little girl," I whispered in her ear.

The taxi drove off, and Via hugged me. We were both crying now.

I went to bed every night and thought about Daisy. It was hard without her. I cried a lot, and Via cried, too.

A few days later, Via came home with three tickets for her school play. "I want you all to come," she said, and she hugged me.

It was my first time at Via's big new school. I sat between Mom and Dad and looked at the **program**. There was a big picture of Justin, and another one of Miranda.

"Why isn't there a picture of Via?" I asked.

"Justin and Miranda have important parts in the play," said Mom. "Via is an understudy."

"What's an understudy?"

"Sometimes an actor gets sick. Then, they have an understudy to take their place."

The play started. Justin came out with his violin, wearing old clothes and a hat.

"This play is *Our Town*, by Thornton Wilder," he said. "The town is Grover's Corners. We begin with a day in our town. It's morning on May 7th 1901."

I knew that I was going to like this play. It felt adult, and not for kids.

A little later in the play, there was a girl called Emily. I knew that Miranda was playing Emily. But I couldn't believe it—it wasn't Miranda, it was Via!

I loved the play, and Via was wonderful. At the end, everyone was **clapping**. Then, Justin and Via came out. Everyone stood up and clapped for a really long time.

After, we went to find Via. She was in a big group, and everyone was smiling and laughing.

"Wow! You were wonderful!" Dad told Via.

He gave her a big hug. Then, Mom hugged her. Mom was so happy that she couldn't speak.

"It was a surprise to see you," said Dad to Via.

"I know," said Via. "Miranda got sick, and I was her understudy."

Then, there were lots of people around us, and for a minute I lost my family. "Via?" I shouted. "Mom!"

"August!" said a voice behind me.

I turned. It was Miranda.

"Good to see you, August," she said, and she hugged me hard.

CHAPTER NINE
The school play

Miranda

My dad left my mom the summer before I went to high school. I didn't see him much after that, and I didn't really want to go to summer camp. But I did go, and it wasn't fun.

After I got home, I called Ella, but I didn't call Via. Ella is an easy friend. She doesn't talk about families and problems, just music and clothes. Via is different, and I didn't want to talk about my parents and their problems. Ella liked my pink hair and my new clothes. I knew that Via didn't.

In high school, Via and I didn't talk much; we just said "Hello."

After a few weeks, I discovered that Via had a boyfriend, Justin: a cute boy with glasses. They were both doing theater, with Mr. Davenport, and I was, too. I wanted the part of Emily in *Our Town*, and so did Via. I was surprised that Mr. Davenport chose me and not her.

Strangely, I started to miss Via and her family. I liked her family, and I loved playing with August.

One day, I called Via's house. I wanted to talk to August.

"Hi, August."

"Miranda!" His voice was happy. "I'm going to school now."

"That's great!" I was surprised. "I hope it's going well."

"It is. I have two new friends: Jack and Summer."

"That's good, August. I miss you," I said. "You know that I'll always be another big sister for you. Call me if you want to, OK? And say hello to Via from me. I miss her, too."

"I will. Bye."

"Bye!"

———

Mom and Dad didn't come to see the play. And there was a big school soccer game that night, so Ella and my other friends went to that. It was evening, and we were all ready to start. I watched people come into the theater, and then I saw August and his parents. I went to see Mr. Davenport.

"Mr. Davenport, I'm sorry," I said. "I can't go on tonight."

"Miranda," he said, "you're just nervous. You'll be OK."

"No, I can't go on. I'm sick."

"OK," he said, and he turned to Justin. "Justin, please find Olivia. She's going to be Emily tonight. Miranda's sick."

I went to the **dressing room** and took off my costume. Via came in.

"Quick," I said. "Put this on! I'm sick. I can't go on."

Via put on the costume, and she looked at me. "You're not sick, Miranda. Why are you doing this?"

Mr. Davenport shouted through the door. "Two minutes, Olivia!"

There was no time to answer.

———————

I saw August after the play. "Good to see you," I said, and I hugged him.

Then, I saw Via and her mom and dad. "How are you?" asked her mom. "Are you sick?"

"I'm OK now, I think," I said.

"We're going to a restaurant," said her dad. "Please come with us."

Via hugged me, and we all walked out of the theater together. I was suddenly very, very happy.

CHAPTER TEN

The camp

August

Every year, in spring, the fifth grade of Beecher Prep goes away for three days and two nights on a camp in Pennsylvania. The kids sleep in **cabins** in the forest. There are camp fires to cook on and long walks in the forest.

We were all excited, but I was also a bit nervous. I've never slept away from home. I've only been in hospital, and then Mom or Dad stayed with me.

Mom helped me to get ready the night before the camp. We chose my clothes, and she put them in my bag.

"What if I can't sleep?" I asked.

"Take a book and a **flashlight**."

She put them in and closed the bag.

"Is it too heavy?" she asked.

"No," I said. "It's OK."

"Time for bed now," she said.

"It's only nine o'clock."

"The bus leaves at six in the morning."

On the bus, I sat next to Jack. Summer and

Maya were in front of us. Miles and Henry got on the bus, but Julian didn't.

"Julian's not coming," I heard Miles saying. I was happy. Three days without Julian would be great. Everyone on the bus was happy and laughing.

We got to the camp about 12 p.m. and put our bags in our cabins. There were six kids in my cabin. Jack and me, and Reid, Tristan, Pablo, and Nino. After lunch, we went for a walk in the forest; the trees were huge. We looked at birds and animals. With my hearing aids I heard the birds really well.

In the evening, we cooked on the camp fire. I loved it—the fire and the dark trees and looking up at the night sky. I was so tired that I went to sleep very quickly.

The next day in the forest was good, too. Then, in the evening we went to another camp for a movie. There were also kids from other schools. We bought food and drink, and Jack, Summer, Reid, Maya, and I all sat together and talked. Suddenly, the lights went out and the movie started.

In the middle of the movie, Jack kicked me.

"Hey, August," he whispered, "I need the restroom."

We went toward the restrooms. There were lots of kids walking around. Some were buying food and drinks. There was a long line at the restrooms.

"I can't wait," said Jack. "Let's go into the forest." We walked toward the trees. We passed Miles, Henry, and Amos. Miles and Henry weren't talking to Jack, but Amos said "Hi."

We were in the trees now, and suddenly we walked into a group of four boys and two girls. They weren't from our school, and I guessed they were in the seventh grade. One of them pointed a flashlight at us.

"What school are you from?" asked a boy.

"Beecher Prep," answered Jack.

Suddenly, one of the girls started shouting. "Oh, no!"

"A freak! A freak!" shouted one of the boys. The light was on my face.

"Let's go," said Jack. He started to walk away, but one of the boys moved in front of us. He was a lot bigger than Jack.

"What's the problem?" asked Jack.

"Your boyfriend's the problem," answered the boy.

Jack took my arm and started to push past the big boy. The boy stopped us and pushed Jack to the ground.

"Hey!" said a voice behind us. "What's the matter?"

The big boy turned and pointed the flashlight toward the voice. It was Amos.

"Leave them," said Amos. Behind him were Miles and Henry.

"More freaks!" shouted the big boy.

"Jack, August, come with us," said Amos. Jack got up, and we started to walk toward Amos. Then, the big boy pulled my sweater, and I fell on to a rock. My arm hurt badly. Amos ran at the boy and hit him hard in the stomach. Someone pulled me up, but another person pulled my sweater again. Then, we got away and we ran out of the trees. The bigger kids didn't follow us.

"We lost the jerks," said Henry.

"You were great," said Jack. "Thanks a lot."

"No problem," said Amos, and he high-fived Jack. Then, Henry and Miles high-fived him. And then they all high-fived me.

"You hurt your arm," said Henry, looking at it.

"It's OK," I said. But it wasn't. It really hurt.

"Wait. Your hearing aids are gone," said Jack.

We all looked for them, but it was dark, and we couldn't see anything.

"It's OK," I said. But that wasn't OK either. I wanted to cry.

We walked back toward the lights. Amos was on my left, and Jack was on my right. Miles was in front and Henry behind.

CHAPTER ELEVEN
Graduation

August

The next morning, Mr. Tushman and some others went back to the forest. They looked for my hearing aids, but they didn't find anything.

"The school will pay for new hearing aids," Mr. Tushman told me. "And we want to find those boys, too. Maybe one of them has your hearing aids."

The bus took us back to school. Mom met me, and she talked to Mr. Tushman. Then, we walked home together. Mom didn't ask me many questions.

It was sad without Daisy at home. Mom hugged me quickly and said, "I missed you, August."

"I missed you, too, Mom. I'm sorry about the hearing aids," I said.

"Don't worry," she said. "Mr. Tushman told me everything. But are you OK?"

"I'm fine. Jack really helped me. And Amos and Henry and Miles! It's strange, because Henry and Miles didn't talk to me all year at school."

"People change," said Mom.

Then, the door opened, and Dad and Via came home. Dad was carrying a box. In the box was a cute little black **puppy**—the cutest puppy I ever saw!

I stayed home the next day with Via, and we played with the puppy all day. It was great to be with Via, talking and laughing. And our puppy was so cute.

The next day, I went back to school, and suddenly everything was different. Everyone knew the story of Jack, Amos, Miles, and Henry and the big seventh grade kids.

Now, everyone liked Amos, Miles, and Henry. And they liked Jack and me, too. And Julian? Nobody was friends with him any more.

In June, the day before the last day of school, Mr. Tushman called me into his office.

"Sit down, August," he said. "Has it been a good year?"

"Yes, it's been good," I said.

"You've studied very hard, and you're one of our best students."

"Thank you."

"I know things were difficult with Julian," he said. How did Mr. Tushman know that?

"Yes, a little," I replied.

"And there were some horrible notes."

"Yes," I said.

"I know," he said. Did Mr. Tushman know *everything*?

"Julian is leaving the school this summer," he added.

I didn't say anything.

He stood up. "Thank you for a good year, August," he said, and we shook hands. "See you at **graduation** tomorrow."

"See you tomorrow, Mr. Tushman."

———

Graduation was in the theater at Beecher Prep Upper School. We all wore our best clothes. Our families and friends were sitting at the back. I sat with Jack and Summer.

Mr. Tushman spoke for a long time, and then some other people spoke. I didn't listen to everything. But then we got to the **medals**, and Mr. Tushman was speaking again.

"The medal for best student goes to Ximena Chin," he said. Ximena went up and got her medal. Charlotte got the medal for music, and Amos got the medal for sports. I was really happy for Amos, because he was now one of my best friends. Then, Summer got the medal for English. Everyone clapped, and they all went up to get their medals.

"There is one more medal," said Mr. Tushman. "The Henry Ward Beecher medal. This medal is for doing something really important for the school. This student has helped a lot of children in the school. He helped them to understand important things about friends. We have all learned from this student. So, August Pullman, please come up and get your medal."

I couldn't believe it. Everyone stood up, clapping and shouting for me. I walked toward Mr. Tushman in a dream. I'm just an ordinary kid, I thought. (But I did finish fifth grade, and that's not easy for anyone.)

Mr. Tushman put the medal over my head. "Well done, August," he whispered.

After graduation, we walked back to our house for cake and ice cream. Jack and his parents, Summer and her mom, Justin, Via, and Miranda, Mom and Dad. I walked behind everybody with Mom.

"Thank you for sending me to school," I said.

"Thank you, August," she said.

"For what?" I said.

"For everything you've given us," she replied. "You really are a **wonder**, August. A wonder."

During-reading questions

Write the answers to these questions in your notebook.

CHAPTER ONE

1 Why has August never been to school?
2 Why don't many people look at August?
3 Why does August have long hair?

CHAPTER TWO

1 How does August feel on his first day at school?
2 Who sits next to August in homeroom?

CHAPTER THREE

1 Why are August and Summer like Beauty and the Beast?
2 Why don't the other children sit next to August in class?

CHAPTER FOUR

1 How are things different for Via on the first day of high school?
2 How does August usually feel about Halloween?
3 Why doesn't August want to go to school after Halloween?

CHAPTER FIVE

1 Why does Summer sit with August every day?
2 What does August tell Summer about Julian and Jack?

CHAPTER SIX

1 Why does Jack agree to help August at school?
2 Who tells Jack about August and Halloween?

CHAPTER SEVEN

1 How is Via's family different from Justin's family?
2 Why are the three boys frightened of Justin?

CHAPTER EIGHT

1 August thinks that Via does not want him to see her play. Why?
2 What is the biggest surprise about the school play?

CHAPTER NINE

1 Why does Miranda find Ella an easier friend than Via?
2 Why does Via have to act in the school play?
3 Why is Miranda happy after the play, do you think?

CHAPTER TEN

1 Why is August worried about going to camp?
2 Who helps Jack and August in the forest?
3 What do the bigger kids in the forest call August and his friends?

CHAPTER ELEVEN

1 What was in the box Dad was carrying?
2 Who is leaving the school in the summer?
3 Who gets the Henry Ward Beecher medal, and why?

After-reading questions

1 Look at the "Before-reading question" on page 6. Which answers did you say were true? Were you right?
2 How does August change in the story? Is he a different person at the end?
3 What changes do you see in Via?
4 Do you think Mr. Tushman and the teachers do enough to help August in school?
5 Jack and Julian both meet August before school starts. What is different about the way that they talk to him?

Exercises

1 **Write the correct words in your notebook.**

1 eastr   _...stare.._ Look at someone hard.
2 plpiaincr   .... The head of a school.
3 dgrae   .... A year at school.
4 mrheoomo   .... The place you go in the morning at school.
5 fiacteera   .... Where you can have lunch at school.
6 odarb   .... A teacher writes on this.
7 vsrenuo   .... Frightened to do something.
8 aaeoixytrrdnr .... Surprising and strange.

2 **Complete these sentences in your notebook, using the words from the box.**

> bowling   complain   problems   Halloween
> mask   camp   nobody   together

1 August wants to go ....*bowling*........ for his birthday.
2 August wears a .... on his face and nobody knows it's him.
3 Via doesn't .... because she's seen August after surgery.
4 The good thing about high school is that .... knows Via.
5 Via knows she has a brother with ....
6 Miranda, Ella, and Via were .... through middle school.
7 Miranda didn't call Via after summer ....
8 August usually loves ....

3 **Match the definitions to the words in your notebook.**

Example: 1–e

1 Something that is not easy   **a** whisper
2 Good to look at   **b** twice
3 Speak very quietly   **c** promise
4 A box that you use to carry something **d** cute
5 Two times   **e** difficulty
6 Say you will do something   **f** case

CHAPTER SIX

4 **Order the sentences by writing *1–7* in the correct order.**

a .... Jack agrees to help.

b .... Jack asks Summer why August is angry with him.

c ....*1*...... Mr. Tushman calls Jack's parents.

d .... Jack and his mom go to see Mr. Tushman.

e .... Jack's mom asks Jack to help the new kid
        at school.

f .... One day, at school, August isn't talking to Jack.

g .... Summer tells Jack about Halloween.

CHAPTER SEVEN

5 **Write the correct words in your notebook.**

1 Via told Justin about August before he *went* / **was going**
   to her house.

2 "Is that a machine gun?" Jack asked Justin. He **looked** /
   was looking at Justin's violin case.

3 Via's parents **invited** / **were inviting** Justin to dinner.

4 Justin really **liked** / **was liking** Via's parents.

5 Jack **wanted** / **was wanting** to buy some candy.

CHAPTER EIGHT

6 Who says these words? Write the correct names in your notebook.

| Via | Jack | August | Mom |

1 "They used pictures of me to make the first Uglydoll!"
........*August*..........

2 "I'm not wearing these, Mom."

3 "You look cool, like a secret policeman."

4 "I don't say anything in the play."

5 "It's not a play for children."

6 "She doesn't want her friends to see a freak."

7 "Via is an understudy."

8 "Miranda got sick."

CHAPTER NINE

7 Order the words to make sentences in your notebook.

1 liked / clothes / hair / my / new / and / pink / Ella / my
Ella liked my pink hair and my new clothes...........................

2 high / didn't / school / talk / in / Via / much / and / I

3 started / to / family / Via / miss / I / her / and

4 be / sister / always / you / another / I'll / big / for

5 evening / it / were / was / ready / to / and / all / start / we

6 to / went / dressing / took / room / the / I / off / and / costume / my

7 was / time / no / there / answer / to

CHAPTER TEN

8 **Match the two parts of the sentences in your notebook.**
Example: 1–c

1 We were all excited,

a and I guessed they were in the seventh grade.

2 We chose my clothes

b and pushed Jack to the ground.

3 With my hearing aids

c but I was also a bit nervous.

4 They weren't from our school

d and hit him hard in the stomach.

5 Jack started to walk away,

e and she put them in my bag.

6 The boy stopped us

f but it was dark, and we couldn't see anything.

7 Amos ran at the boy

g I heard the birds really well.

8 We all looked for my hearing aids,

h but one of the boys moved in front of us.

CHAPTERS ONE TO ELEVEN

9 **Write the correct form of the verbs in your notebook.**

1 August **was having** / *has had* a lot of plastic surgery.

2 Via **was always being** / **has always been** friends with Miranda and Ella.

3 Miranda **has known** / **have known** August for years.

4 "Julian **was turning** / **has turned** the whole class against me," said Jack.

5 The world **was** / **has been** cruel to August.

6 August **has never heard** / **was never hearing** very well, and now he needs hearing aids.

7 August **was never sleeping** / **has never slept** away from home.

8 "You **were studying** / **have studied** very hard," Mr. Tushman said to August.

Project work

1 Some of the people in August's class wrote precepts.
Read them, and then write your own precept.
Charlotte's precept: It's not enough to be friendly.
You have to be a friend.
Henry's precept: Don't be friends with jerks.
Julian's precept: Sometimes it's good to start over.
Summer's precept: If you can get through middle school
without hurting anyone, that's really cool.
Your precept: . . .

2 There are chapters in this book by August, Via, Summer,
Jack, Justin, and Miranda, but there isn't a chapter by
Julian. Write this chapter, using 150–250 words. Include
some of these things:

• the first time you see August and show him the school
• the first day at school, when Jack sits next to August
• Halloween, and August's mask
• when Jack hits you
• the letter from Jack
• the "war" with Jack and August
• the meeting with Justin and his "machine gun" (violin).

3 If you can, watch the movie of *Wonder*. What is different
about the movie? Why did they make these changes, do you
think? Do you like the movie more, or the book? Why?

Glossary

Beauty and the Beast (pr. n.)
a story about a beautiful girl
(= the *beauty*) and a large ugly
animal (= the *beast*)

board (n.)
A teacher writes on a *board*. It is
on the classroom wall.

bone (n.)
You have *bones* in your body.
They are strong, hard and white.

bowling (n.)
Bowling is a game. You throw
a heavy ball toward ten things
that look like bottles.

boyfriend (n.)
a man or a boy who is special to
you. You love or like him a lot.

cabin (n.)
a small house in the mountains
or in a forest

cafeteria (n.)
a restaurant in a school or
hospital. You buy your food and
take it to a table.

call (v.)
You *call* someone with a phone.

camp (n.)
Children go on holiday to a *camp*,
often without their parents.

case (n.)
A *case* is a special box. You use it
for carrying things.

clap (v.)
to hit your hands together to
show that you like something

complain (v.)
to say that you are not happy
about something

cool (adj.)
Cool people look and sound good.

costume (n.)
clothes that you wear to a special
party; for example, you wear a
Spider-Man *costume*.

cruel (adj.)
Cruel people are not kind.

cute (adj.)
A *cute* person looks nice.

difficulty (n.)
a problem

dressing room (n.)
You change your clothes in
a *dressing room*.

extraordinary (adj.)
very different, and better
than normal

flashlight (n.)
a small light. You carry it in the dark.

four square (n.)
a game for four people. They play it with a ball.

freak (n.)
A *freak* is not a normal person. *Freak* is not a kind word.

go out with (phr. v.)
You *go out with* a person. You love or like them a lot.

grade (n.)
At school, most children in a *grade* are about the same age. Children in fifth *grade* are usually ten or eleven years old.

graduation (n.)
Graduation is a special day. It is the last day of this school for you.

Halloween (n.)
the night of October 31st. Children wear strange or funny clothes and go to houses in their street. People give them candy.

hearing aid (n.)
a small thing that people wear in their ear. It helps them to hear better.

high-five (v.)
People *high-five* to say hello. They put their hand above their head and touch the other person's hand.

homeroom (n.)
You go to your *homeroom* at school in the morning. There is a teacher in the *homeroom*.

hug (v.)
to put your arms around a person because you love or like them

invite (v.)
to ask a person to come to your party

jerk (n.)
a word for a stupid person. *Jerk* is not a kind word.

kid (n.)
a child

mask (n.)
You wear a *mask* over your face.

math (n.)
You learn *math* at school. *Math* is about numbers.

medal (n.)
You win a *medal* for doing something very well. It is small, flat and round.

miss (a person) (v.)
You are sad because a person is not with you. You *miss* the person.

nervous (adj.)
worried because you think that something bad will happen

note (n.)
paper with a message on it

ordinary (adj.)
normal, and not special or different

plague (n.)
In this story, the *plague* is a child's word for something bad that makes you ill. They think they will get it from touching another person.

plastic surgery (n.)
A doctor does *plastic surgery* on a person's face or body to change it and make it better.

play (n.)
A *play* is when people act a story at a theater.

principal (n.)
the most important teacher in a school

program (n.)
At a *play*, a *program* is a piece of paper or a small book. It gives you information about the *play*.

promise (v.)
1. to say something is true. 2. to say that you will do something. Then, you must do it.

puppy (n.)
a very young dog

science (n.)
You learn *science* at school. *Science* is about the world around us.

shake (v.)
to move quickly from side to side or up and down. You *shake* a person's hand to say hello.

stare (v.)
to look at a person for a long time

text (v.)
to send a message using a cell phone

throw up (phr. v.)
to be ill. Food or drink comes out your mouth.

violin (n.)
You play music on a *violin*. You put it against your neck and move a long, thin thing across it.

war (n.)
fighting between countries or
groups of people

whisper (v.)
to speak very quietly

witch (n.)
In stories, a *witch* is an ugly, bad
person. She wears black clothes
and does bad things.

wonder (n.)
a very unusual and good thing
or person